DON'T FORGET the TOILET PAPER

[and 24 Other Rules for Real Estate]

by

Former Realtor, Gerry Clare

Copyright © 2011 Gerry Clare
All rights reserved.

Illustrations by: Chris Fenoglio

ISBN: 0615429106
ISBN-13: 9780615429106

Biographical information

The author recounts from personal experience as a Realtor for almost twenty years in three states, and as a customer service professional for another twelve years, some of her experiences in real estate and what they taught her. She was Rookie of the Year, Realtor of the Year, and President of her Association of Realtors organization most recently and is a licensed real estate instructor.

Her insight on the industry since the 1970s when she began her career to 2005 when she retired is meant to be a guide for anyone interested in the profession or as insight into the industry for nonprofessionals.

After reading this manuscript, one of her friends, who is not in real estate, was amazed at all the facets of the business. Certainly, the agents she worked with have many stories to add. Purposefully, she has omitted sad stories and tried to see the positive sides of all experiences.

Most of all, she loved the challenges of the profession, the people and agents she met along the way. She is profoundly thankful to her first Florida brokers, Joan Bond and Barbara Lyle, who made her take training courses in Florida; to her patient husband, Tom, who pushed her back into the business; her daughter, Jennifer, for her encouragement (who is now an independent business owner herself); and all her friends who read this manuscript and chuckled. Of course, I would be remiss if I didn't thank my most recent broker, Janie Westmoreland, for all her advice and my wonderful partner and friend, Kathy White, for her continuing professionalism and making our jobs a fun adventure. A special thanks to Maureen Jung for her suggestions to reorganize this manuscript into a possible positive guide for real estate professionals.

TABLE OF CONTENTS

Chapter 1
Starting Out (New Jersey 1970–1973)   1

Rule #1 – Get Organized   2
Rule #2 – Call Your Mother   3
Rule #3 – Write Down Your Goals   5
Rule #4 – Farm Your Neighborhood   6
Rule #5 – Don't Mix Business and Home   7
Rule #6 – Keep Good Records   9
Rule #7 – Attend Open Houses and Realtor Caravans   11
Rule #8 – Don't Forget the Toilet Paper   12

Chapter 2
Next In My Career – Pittsburgh (1973–1976)   15

Rule #9 – Learn the Area   15
Rule #10 – Don't Take Cash in a Paper Bag   16
Rule #11 – Interview Your Buyers and Sellers   18

Chapter 3
Back in New Jersey – Hiatus in My
Real Estate Career (1977–1987)   21

Rule #12 – Don't Work Part-Time   21

Chapter 4
Finally in Florida – Back to Real Estate (1994–2006)   23

Rule #13 – Don't Be a Property Manager…Unless   23
Rule #14 – Join the Community – Volunteer   25
Rule #15 – Branding – Rent a Cherry Picker   26
Rule #16 – Specialize in the "Unusual"   27
Rule #17 – Get Educated – Go to Vegas   28
Rule #18 – Dress the Part   30
Rule #19 – Make Lots of Noise   31
Rule #20 – Do Open Houses – Offer Ice Cream   34

Chapter 5
Final Thoughts…Until the Next Book   37

Rule #21 – Be Ethical – Heed Your Conscience   37
Rule #22 – Employ Your Relatives and Consult a Tax Specialist 39
Rule #23 – Take a Vacation – Have Some Fun   40
Rule #24 – Attending the Home Inspection – Yes or No   42
Rule #25 – Know When to Retire   44

CHAPTER I

Starting Out (New Jersey 1970–1973)

It all started when we bought our first house in the early '70s. My husband had just started a new job after completing his military duty in the Coast Guard. Our three-year-old daughter was in day care and I was working for a large company in New Jersey.

"Don't worry, we're not going to buy anything," I told my husband. "We're just going to look. I don't even have the checkbook with me. Let's just take a peek at the possibilities."

In the future a Realtor friend of mine in Florida would categorize this outlook as "not serious buyers" or "looky Lou's."

Needless to say, we bought a house that day with $1 down—fifty cents of that borrowed from the Realtor. It was a little Cape Cod with radiant heat in the floors and a half-finished upstairs, purchased with VA no-down-payment financing for $36,000.

The day we closed was during Thanksgiving week and I decided to invite both sets of parents for the turkey day itself, our first real party. It was a great idea, but the oven died and we learned how to smoke a turkey on the charcoal grill.

The house was all ours (and the bank's). Shortly after we closed, the broker of our salesman's firm approached me with the Century 21 "gold" jacket, promising me a great career in real estate. I decided this was the profession for me. After all, my husband provided the primary income, so I had a little leeway, as the pay was by commission only.

So I took the crash thirty-day real estate licensing course at Berg Real Estate School and graduated with lots of trepidation and dreams of becoming rich. I soon found out that real estate in the '70s in my new office meant eight guys sitting around, waiting for the phone to ring with sellers to list their properties and buyers to go looking for theirs.

These early experiences led to several universal tried and true basics of getting started in the real estate profession and I have listed them in the following pages. I have also included an *Action Item* and *Date* completed section after each suggestion for the real estate rookie to use as needed.

Rule #1 – Get Organized – *Set up your work area.*

OK, so we had three-ring binders with pull-out listings of houses for sale in our area from the multiple listing service, followed by daily bulletins of price changes, "solds," etc. to amend each sheet. You really had to keep your binder current, or risk total embarrassment when you relied on the info, or called the sellers for an appointment. At that time all agents worked for the sellers and things were pretty simple, leading to the statement "buyer beware." Also, setting up client cards, daily time schedules for appointments, and working with maps to set up geographic showings were important parts of the daily routine. Today, of course, we have computers, Palm Pilots, cell phones, and GPS mapping for instant help and communications.

The principles are still the same today. You need to set up your workspace whether at home, the office, or both. You will probably be meeting customers or clients at your real estate office, so meet with your broker to discuss layout and professional tools available to you. Will you be using a laptop (portable) or desktop computer in the office? At home? Will you need an iPhone or PDA to access the multi-list while you are showing property? Do you have GPS in your car? Will you need a lockbox key for inventory?

Don't forget to ask about your personal or company signs as well. Your professional association of Realtors may also supply certain items for you. Take good notes and observe how others in the office operate. Ask their opinions if needed.

....
Action Item – Rule #1 – Meet broker to discuss tools needed and office setup.
Date: _____
....

Rule #2 – Call Your Mother – *and everyone you know.*

I started out by making a list of everyone I knew and sending out letters with my business card. I followed up with a phone call to ask friends from those lists or anyone to go with me to open houses or showings, so I could practice. In other words, unlike others in my office, I could not afford to sit and wait for the phone to ring, unless I was on floor duty and had to answer the phones.

This strategy worked for me then, and I feel should still work in the current market. Think about everyone you see during an average week while driving kids to school or after-school events and going to the hair salon, doctors' and dentists' offices, social clubs, church, and fitness centers. Then write those names down. You are actually starting your mailing list.

You may not want to do a mass mailing to everyone in these groups. Just select friends from these groups and your neighborhood to start. Make a list with addresses and phone numbers, as you will want to follow up soon after you send your letter or postcard.

....

Action Item 1 – Rule #2 – Make a list.
Date: _____

Action Item 2 – Rule #2 – Mail out.
Date: _____

Action Item 3 – Rule #2 – Call
Date: _____

....

Rule #3 – Write Down Your Goals – *and review at least quarterly.*

I have always been a list maker. Ever since college, I found it easier to make lists and check things off when they are done. This was just natural for me; although, when starting out, it is necessary to meet with your broker or sales manager to figure out what is and is not realistic. Keep goals to an achievable number.

There are many books about writing down your goals, breaking them down timewise, and reviewing them regularly, so I am not going to go too deeply into this rule. This really helped me evaluate annually where my best efforts went and into which direction I should be heading for the following year. For example, I made charts, one for sellers and one for buyers, and noted where I got the client, marital status, male or female, age, price of sale and any other data that helped me identify my "ideal" client. (Note: Of course, these first clients also went on my mailing list to stay in touch with a call or note.)

If you were wildly successful the first year and you didn't follow your goals, throw them out and improve on what you did for the following year. If you weren't successful, re-evaluate them with professional help, i.e., with a broker or manager.

Later in my career, I also learned that I needed to codify personal goals as well. I realized how few times I was home on time or for dinner before 8:00 p.m. and how little time I was spending with friends and family. One of my goals then was to have lunch or coffee once a week with a friend.

....

Action Item 1 – Rule #3 – Meet with your broker for first-year goals.
Date: _____

Action Item – Rule #3 – Make buyers/sellers sales chart.
Date: _____

Action Item 3 – Rule #3 – Evaluate and write new goals.
Date: _____

....

Rule #4 – Farm Your Neighborhood

My first broker actually expected me to knock on doors and cold call in my neighborhood to start. It was, after all, a simpler time in the 1970s. Fortunately, most people were not home, what with two-income families even then. But I did start a mail campaign in my neighborhood, introducing myself, and following up with phone calls.

This generated some leads and added to my mailing list. Past buyers and sellers (see Rule #3) as well as "calling everyone you know" (Rule #2) combined with the names from your farming neighborhood can help you create your mailing list as well. Cultivate your farm by sending out a real estate newsletter, community announcements or news of events affecting real estate, postcards with new and sold listings, or any regular mailing that will remind people that you are still in the real estate business.

I found this type of farming more effective than picking one subdivision and bombarding it with mail. However, it makes sense if you do a lot of business in one area to brand yourself as the specialist for that area. Later on, when there aren't as many sales in that farm you can just adopt another where there is more activity.

....

Action Item 1 – Rule #4 – Designate a farming area
Date: _____

Action Item 2 – Rule #4 – Develop a newsletter or regular mailing.
Date: _____

Action Item 3 – Rule #4 – Do follow-up mailings with calls.
Date: _____

....

Rule #5 – Don't Mix Business and Home….(And don't leave Tuffy in the drawer.)

Our daughter was three or four years old when I started my new career in real estate. I remember trying hard to balance home, day care, and work like most working mothers. Fortunately, I didn't have to depend on my income alone to support us, so I was able to work more nights and weekends when hubby was home than during the work week when I needed to be available for her.

Occasionally, I would just "stop by the office" for a minute to pick up a contract or make some calls. At first Jennifer thought it was fun. She got to sit at my desk or play with my office supplies. However, my "minute" more often than not, could stretch into an hour.

But the icing on the cake involved "Tuffy," my daughter's Christmas present. Tuffy walked and barked even though he was a stuffed dog and Jennifer adored him. When he got "sick" and stopped walking altogether, I told her that I would take Tuffy to the animal hospital where he would certainly recover.

Unfortunately, in the rush of my hectic schedule, I dumped poor Tuffy in my bottom desk drawer and forgot all about him. Well, one fateful day, when Jen and I stopped by the office for a "few minutes," she opened my large desk drawer.

My name was "mud."

"What is Tuffy doing in your office," she cried. "I thought he was in the animal hospital."

Quite honestly, I was so traumatized that I don't remember my snappy comeback, if I even had one. I just know that this was a big moment in our relationship. I wonder today if it was the defining one and, in fact, even worse than when she discovered Santa was wearing her Uncle Bob's shoes.

I do know that somehow this lesson was meant to try to keep office and home separate. Of course, this is me talking now; I continued to "stop by the office" throughout my career, getting involved for more time than anticipated.

My daughter managed to pay me back when I visited her in California recently. She said we could "do lunch" as soon as she checked some things at the office. So, around 1:00 p.m. I called her, as I had locked myself out of the house while walking her dog. She said she got tied up and forgot the time. After all, this was her business and she was the responsible owner. She has her own graphic arts business and I suspect she is somewhat of a perfectionist too. (She doesn't get that from me, does she?)

But I really get that responsibility thing. We both probably take ourselves too seriously. We had lunch around three o'clock and it was OK too.

Action Item 1 – Rule #5 – At the beginning of each week, plan out office and home hours as much as possible.
Date: _____

Action Item 2 – Rule #5 – Don't bring children to the office unless they are working for you and money.
Date: _____

Rule #6 – Keep Good Records

When I started my real estate career in New Jersey, there was no e-mail. Having been an executive secretary in my previous life, I recognized the importance of keeping good notes and annotating my files.

In real estate, on a daily basis, there are many crucial decisions to be made, especially when signing listing agreements and purchase and sale contracts. Changes along the way need to be dated and signed by all parties affected. Today, confirming e-mails make the task much easier and improve communications between all parties to the contracts.

My early first challenge to the "he said-she said" conflict came when I got a frantic call from my engineer client who was on the site of his new home being built in the subdivision we were handling for the builder.

"My house is gold," he yelled into the phone.

While I tried to regroup and pull his file, he continued to expound on the problem by adding, "So is the house next door."

Now I knew something was wrong, even though his file called for gold and was initialed in my folder, there were not supposed to be two homes with the same color next to each other. Fully grasping the problem, I tried to calm him down and note that indeed, he was correct, and I would call the builder.

Although this was a relatively inexpensive fix, rectified by a coat of paint, this could have been much worse. I learned that having all the choices for a new home, initialed by the builder and buyer in a current file, solved problems that could come up along the way.

Years later in my one mediation case, these file notes became even more crucial. E-mails, listing and contract changes, and extensions have now become common support paperwork in each transaction file, as well as the modern requirements for representation agreements. The representation statement defines the agreed upon roles of the selling and buying agents and the need for them, now regulated by the individual states. The seller's disclosure deals with the condition of the property, also state regulated.

I often made notes of meetings or agreements for the file with backup paperwork, initialed or not, as needed. If you are ever called up in front of your Board's Grievance Committee, you will also be very thankful for a time line or notes to help your memory. Often a lot of time passes between an incident and a hearing.

Action Item 1 – Rule #6 – Set up an e-mail file on phone, voice recorder, or laptop for daily personal notes on client meetings/phone conversations.

Date: _____

Action Item 2 – Rule #6 – Print as needed and file in office record file.

Date: _____

Rule #7 – Attend Open Houses and Realtor Caravans

This is only common sense. Know the inventory. I started attending open houses and Realtors' caravans, as I didn't have much else on my schedule. It paid off when the sister of the gal who replaced me at my old company actually went with me to a house I saw on caravan earlier in the week for my first showing. She and her hubby decided to become my first sale and consequently, listing, as well. I was off and running, and life was good.

Open houses held by Realtors not only help you to know the inventory, but also label you as a professional. When you go to list a house or show another one in the neighborhood where you checked out an open house, you can exhibit expertise and knowledge of your product. In many cases your customers or prospective sellers will already have seen that house or use it incorrectly as a comparable.

Attending "for sale by owner" open houses can introduce you to a potential seller/client as well. Being sincerely interested in them and their home, by making some useful suggestions, if asked, can also add to your professional image. I even attended builders' open houses to stay current on new models and prices. I sometimes have picked up a referral from a builder's representative at the site, especially on a Sunday when many real estate offices do not have regular hours.

Many areas have Realtor Caravans, which, as I mentioned, help you keep up with the inventory, but also enable you to establish a good relationship with other Realtors you may be working with on future transactions.

Action Item 1 – Rule #7 – Attend open house by For Sale by Owner (FSBO).
Date: _____

Action Item 2 – Rule #7 – Attend builder's open house.
Date: _____

Action Item 3 – Rule #7 – Attend Realtor's Caravan.
Date: _____

Rule #8 – Don't Forget the Toilet Paper

This is a good rule, especially if you are way out in the woods, sitting a model home all day and there is no toilet paper in the bathroom. Gee, the boys in the office never mentioned that. Thank goodness for "Out to Lunch" signs and nearby gas stations.

Seriously though, sitting open houses and model homes for builders was an ideal way to gather buyers and sellers as well. Besides the toilet paper, when you are away from the office, keep a good supply of necessary listing and contract forms, a guest roster, and book of active listings (or, like today, your laptop), so you can establish your relationship with a potential client or customer right at the site.

I actually went to talk to a client's friend about listing his acreage. He told me to meet him in the cornfield and I thought, "How cool, now I'll get to see the property." So I worked up some comps on the property as listed in the tax rolls and headed out in my Jeep—up the main road and down the dirt road where I saw him standing by his truck.

We chatted awhile and he surprised me by telling me "to sign him up." My office was fifteen miles away and he was obviously ready now, so I whipped out the listing contract, half filled out and completed on the hood of the car. He signed it and I stuck the sign up on the main road as I left.

Again, the same lesson prevails...be prepared. I already had my buyers and sellers binder in my car (before laptops), all the listing and contract forms, the signs and, of course, toilet paper for emergencies. Today, even with the technological advances, it is still advisable to have all your backup tools with you, including copies of listings you are showing, and other forms for buyers and sellers, copies when the Internet fails.

Action Item 1 – Rule #8 – Check supply of forms in car/briefcase weekly.
Date: _____

CHAPTER 2

Next In My Career – Pittsburgh (1973–1976)

I barely got started in New Jersey in my career, when we moved to Pittsburgh for my husband's job and it was back to school for more credits (in real estate law) and relicensing. OK, so my snobby friends in the New York City metropolitan area wanted to throw us a "funeral" party when they heard where we were moving. I think they had visions of smoke-belching steel mills, smoke-filled bars, and scenes from the movie *The Deer Hunter*. I confess I had no idea what to expect.

However, when we got there, I knew I couldn't sell real estate in an area I really didn't know at all, nor appreciate, thanks to our naysaying friends.

Rule #9 – Learn the Area

So I began to tour the area, asking my new neighbors what they liked about Pittsburgh. Wow, there's the Heinz ketchup factory, the zoo, the state and county parks and hilly golf courses, the Incline, the downtown area with Three Rivers Stadium, the Cathedral of Learning, and many great ethnic restaurants and bars.

The list was endless and I did it all (except they didn't have the ketchup tour anymore). All the while, I was watching the cleanup of the rivers, factories, and steel mill pollution, while learning the streets and neighborhoods I needed to know in the South Hills. I got my Pennsylvania real estate sales license and started working for a broker in a very small office on the border of Mt. Lebanon, Upper St. Clair (there was no Lower St. Clair, to my knowledge), and Bethel Park in the South Hills area of Pittsburgh.

Again, this was before GPS, but just driving through the various neighborhoods, snapping pictures for my "buyers and sellers books," made me more comfortable with knowing values and directions. Locating schools, landmarks, churches, parks, and shopping became a daily adventure. Today, Google can help with all that.

Action Item 1 – Rule #9 – Take pictures and drive through various neighborhoods and subdivisions.
Date: _____

Rule #10 – Don't Take Cash in a Paper Bag

We were there only a few years before my husband again took a new job out of state. However, I learned several valuable lessons in my short career there. Our office was small, so I did get some good "up calls" on duty. In fact, one of my first walk-ins looked like he may have just walked down the mall from the tavern at the other end of the strip, so I wasn't so sure about his motivation.

I did my usual interview to match his "buyer" needs to our inventory, but he seemed very focused on not providing me with his personal information. We set up an appointment to preview one of our listings later that evening. I took my husband with me when I met him that night on the way into Pittsburgh where we were attending a party. Hubby sat in the car while we walked the property and, as we left, the buyer handed me a small paper bag with cash in it to hold the house until his wife could see it the next day.

The next day he brought his wife (that was a relief) to see the house. She actually didn't like it, but she and I proceeded to find the perfect "estate" for her and the kids and we kept the money for the deposit and filled out the contract. Years later I found out there were some good reasons for all the deception, but I am still sworn to secrecy and maintain contact with the wife until this day.

Later I was told to be suspicious of cash in a paper bag by my shocked broker. Fortunately we had discussed the fact that deposits had to be turned over to the broker immediately the next morning.

Action Item 1 – Rule #10 – Meet with the broker and discuss rules of deposits and escrows for your state.
Date: _____

Rule #11 – Interview Your Buyers and Sellers

When I first started in real estate, whoever called on the phone or walked in the door was "mine." It became my personal challenge to convert every "prospect" into customer or client.

I had a charming listing with a greenhouse in the country of the South Hills area. The sellers were a wonderful couple who were scaling down and retiring. The buyers were a young businessman on the rise and his wife who called in on my floor duty. After we drew up a mutually agreeable contract and it was fully executed, the buyers started pressing me to go back to look at the house repeatedly, mostly with short notice to the sellers.

After they received their letter of mortgage approval (and interest rates at this time were in double digits), the endless visits and demands to change and add things to the contract began. Finally, the sellers had had enough and stood firm with the contract as written, even though I advised them, the buyers might start figuring out a way to get out of it.

Sure enough, when I explained to the buyers, that the sellers were frustrated with their demands, they decided they wanted to get out of the contract and have their deposit returned. The sellers were actually fine with this, as they now really did not want these people (him primarily) to live in their beloved house. They released the buyers from the contract. The buyers then asked me to find them something else, and I suggested they might work better with another Realtor.

The house above sold very quickly, as it was a unique and lovely property, and I learned a valuable lesson: screen buyers and sellers more closely. If they are not motivated, realistic in their needs, and feel comfortable with you, then you will probably avoid a lot of hassle in the future and even possible legal complications by rejecting them. Although a good option, I now realize, would be to refer them to another Realtor and, at least get a referral fee, especially if you have worked with them extensively and been unable to communicate. You can always refer them to someone you don't like?

Only kidding.

Years later I was having lunch with a few friends and one of them said, "You must have had a lot of strange clients and customers."

After thinking about it, I had to admit that there were a few, but the majority of them were fine people—many became future friends. "Maybe," I replied, "this was because I learned a little from the unhappy buyers in Pittsburgh or maybe because the only people who stuck with me were interviewing me as well, and that's why we clicked and respected each other's opinions."

Moving can be a very stressful time and we, as professionals, need to work to make the clients and customers as comfortable with the adjustment as possible. We were only in Pittsburgh for a few years, when my husband announced another career move to Findlay, Ohio, south of Toledo, and the home of Marathon Oil and Cooper Tire. We were only here for about a year, just enough time for me to go back to school for another new required law course and take my real estate exam again in Columbus.

Action Item 1 – Rule #11 – Develop two brief interview sheets with qualifying questions for buyers and sellers.
Date: _____

CHAPTER 3

Back in New Jersey – Hiatus in My Real Estate Career (1977–1987)

I really never worked in my real estate office in Ohio, except to sell my own house, as my world fell apart with an unexpected divorce. My dad (who was living with us), my daughter, and I moved back to New Jersey where I had family, friends, and prospects of a job with a steady salary, which I needed as a single parent with little child support.

Rule #12 – Don't Work Part-Time

After we were settled back in New Jersey, my first visit was to my old real estate office to see if I still fit in my gold Century 21 jacket. My first broker thought I would do well as a sales manager on weekends and in sales part time so that I would have some steady income. He still represented a well-known builder exclusively and the previous sales manager had quit.

I thought about it for a while but figured it just wasn't fair to work nights and weekends as a single parent. So, I returned to work with a previous employer and worked myself up in the customer service field to a customer service manager with a major worldwide company in just six years. Also I was paid a salary plus benefits, bonuses, and stock options. I continued my customer service career in Seattle, when my new husband moved there for a career transfer.

However, reflecting on many part-time Realtors working in Florida, I would say that associates who worked part-time seemed to make exactly that—a part-time income. On the other hand, full-time successful agents worked overtime to develop their businesses and made the top dollars.

Later, after I retired, I taught the real estate licensing course, and I realized there was another group of part-time agents who made money and they were the investors. They bought, managed, and sold their own properties, collecting commissions or negotiating them along the way. That would be a definite exception to rule #12.

....

Action Item 1 – Rule #12 – Consider pros and cons of part-time work before entering a real estate career.
Date_____

....

CHAPTER 4

Finally in Florida – Back to Real Estate (1994–2006)

After getting married again and living in Seattle for five years, we moved to beautiful Amelia Island, Florida, and lived right on the Atlantic Ocean for five years. We did a lot of boating. My husband loved the golf and also took care of his dad who moved in with us until he passed away.

It was too early for me to retire and our kids were grown and on their own, so I worked for a while with the US Chamber of Commerce in Jacksonville, having transferred from the Seattle office. But, I hated the traveling and my husband encouraged me to go back into real estate.

I was reluctant to get back in the grind and hard work to once again start over on a small island with over one hundred Realtors and a population of only ten thousand. I could see with the opening of the Ritz Carlton and the second home resort business, that the market was growing. So, I was back to school in Jacksonville, taking my test in Orlando. My husband gallantly took the course and test with me. Once again, we were in business.

Rule #13 – Don't Be a Property Manager Unless…

We thought property management might be the way to start and I took a course at the local community college. We started working with a company on the island, hoping for regular hours and a steadier salary. We were the Tom (my husband) and Gerry property management team in 1995 and worked on short- and long-term rentals.

I took in the money, showed the properties, and did the paperwork. Tom did all the hard stuff, setting up the new computer, delivering keys, unstopping toilets, and putting up signs. Here is why I say, "Don't be a property manager unless…you have really tough skin."

The landlords are never happy, because there are always more repairs and less of a proceeds check than they expected. The tenants are never happy because they are just never satisfied. On the opposite side of the spectrum when you are working with buyers and sellers, they are almost always happy, especially the day they move in or the day they receive the proceeds of the sale. Not only that, most transactions last only thirty to ninety days, where property management relationships can go on forever.

Of course, I do remember one fairly humorous event before we left that venture. I worked in an open office during the day that housed several real estate-related services and agents who were normally busy on the phone. When my phone rang, I picked it up and the office was oddly silent at that moment. I started answering the customer's questions about a rental property, and said, "No, I'm sorry but you cannot have a cow on that particular property."

My office buddies started muffled giggling, while I had to then remark, "Oh, no, I'm sorry, you can't have a chow either." That did it…giggling became out and out guffawing. But, that's not why we left and I went into sales again. First of all, my partner quit or I fired him, whichever version you believe, and second, a great couple from Blowing Rock, North Carolina, walked into the office one day to look at property when no salespeople were in the office. So, I did the deed and realized that is where I belonged…back with the challenge of the needs of the buyers versus the inventory provided by the sellers.

....

Action Item 1 – Rule #13 – Talk to a property manager before entering that career.
Date_____

Action Item 2 – Rule #13 – Take a property management course if you decide to proceed.
Date_____

....

Rule #14 – Join the Community – Volunteer

I was new in my sales career once again, and so I began to join community organizations: driving for the American Cancer Society, working on a local Chamber committee, attending the ABWA meetings (American Business Woman's Association) and dancing with the local social dance club. Of course, I also joined Newcomers, as I was a newcomer. Later, a friend persuaded me to be on an ad hoc city committee to restore an old school building into a community center. This involved trips to Tallahassee for funding and running a local talent show for five years. All in all, I made lots of contacts and enjoyed working in the community as well. One caution, though: if you get involved in your local Realtor organization, try not to be president of that group and ABWA and in charge of a Chamber committee at the same time.

Getting involved in the community and with fellow Realtors is valuable in the long run. I was getting educated and working with other Realtors, which helped in dealings later down the line and resulted in valuable contacts as well.

Once again, I was attending every open house and Caravan to learn the inventory and neighborhoods. When you don't have a lot of customers, this is easy to do.

....

Action Item 1 – Rule #14 – Make a list of community organizations that you are interested in and would best fit your professional or personal interests.
Date_____

Action Item 2 – Rule #14 – Do not be an officer of more than one group at a time.
Date_____

....

Rule #15 – Branding – Rent a Cherry Picker.

I'm six feet tall, so I thought that "Rising to the Challenge" was a good slogan for me and I used it everywhere…on my business cards, ads, and my personal brochure. I had a neat three-story contemporary listing across the street from the ocean and decided that I needed some unusual ad photos. I rented a bucket truck from a local electrician and took a "For Sale" sign up in the cherry picker to the third story to take some photos, while my patient and supportive husband took pictures of me and my sign, "rising to the challenge."

A few years later I updated my photo and climbed up a ladder in a business suit….a much cleaner more professional image. I used these photos on newsletters, thank you notes, signs, my car, news releases, and any publicity or mail-outs I used. I have even seen others' faces on billboards and benches, although I never went that far.

As a sidenote, I learned from experience that using a professional photographer can enhance your publicity and make you look more professional. If you want to be known as a tennis player, and that is the image you want to convey, then go for it, but consider what you are trying to say with your photo. And please, do not use a twenty-year-old photo or a glamour shot. I think you get the idea.

....

Action Item 1 – Rule #15 – Pick your professional photo and brand.
Date_____

Action Item 2 – Rule #15 – Run it by your broker.
Date_____

....

Rule #16 – Specialize in the "Unusual"

Before I moved to Florida, I had never seen a mobile home. However, there weren't too many Realtors fighting over those listings, and they were very reasonably priced. They were located mostly off our island, where the necessary acre zoning existed. I quickly learned the geography of "off island" and began to work these areas.

When my associates wanted to know where a street on the mainland was (before GPS and Google earth), they asked me. Now everyone knows where everything is, thanks to the Internet. My average sale was under $80,000 and it took a lot of sales and hard work to earn my million dollar plaque, Rookie of the Year, and Realtor of the Year. On the other hand, my customers were mostly first-time buyers and very loyal, providing referrals regularly.

Many were ready for a stick-built home several years later. Working in a steadily increasing value market made these customers a great start for me in a new area. You might even approach a large employer or local military base to specialize in those customers. Find a niche...it may even be condos or lakefront property.

....

Action Item #1 – Rule #16 – Look for the unusual market and specialize.
Date_____

....

Rule #17 – Get Educated – Go to Vegas

To repeat, when you are not flooded with customers or clients, go for all the professional education you can. I started my GRI (Graduate Realtors Institute) classes the first time they were offered in nearby Jacksonville, which included my first two-year license renewal requirement.

I attended every educational class at our board and some in Jacksonville, networking and learning as well. I even attended a "Homes and Land" magazine seminar on Web design and bought one of the early Web sites in our area. It was linked to their national real estate magazine, earning me extra publicity and referrals. My favorite feature of this Web site was that I could add my new listings immediately with my new digital camera and had immediate and easy access to my site.

Several years in a row, a group of us from Amelia Island even attended our state Legislative Day in Tallahassee. This was not only a good networking experience, as we tagged along with the larger

Jacksonville contingent, but it helped us see the relationship of laws that affect our housing industry.

I saved up some money and went to my first RE/MAX convention to get the bigger picture of my company. Fortunately, it was in Las Vegas, somewhere I had never been. My husband and another couple joined me and we had a great old time. I actually attended several workshops and watched the big award agents walk across the stage (I opted to pick up my little award later). It was a great motivating experience and fun besides.

Attending our state convention in Florida was equally profitable, and not nearly as expensive, as several of us carpooled and only stayed over one night.

I noticed that the nature of the typical real estate office from the 1970s to the 1980s changed from mostly men to mostly women. The 1980s to the 1990s brought in retirees in a second career, and young business majors (men and women) out of college. It is definitely more of a mix in many offices today in our area. However, it is also still true that the longer you are in the business the more successful you can be. Because there are more and more referrals, there are still probably more older agents.

Speaking of education, a psychology degree would probably be an excellent course to pick up in dealing with sellers, buyers, and motivation. I know I wish I had picked up a course along the way.

Action Item 1 – Rule #17 – Sign up for a GRI or other Realtor designation course.
Date_____

Action Item 1 – Rule #17 – Sign up for a real estate convention.
Date_____

Rule #18 – Dress the Part

Working in business and customer service for ten years before real estate meant wearing suits (no pants), panty hose, and heels for me. We're talking the '60s, '70s, and into the '80s here, folks. But moving on through the years from the mustard gold Century 21 jacket in New Jersey to less formal markets in Pittsburgh, Ohio, and finally Florida (Amelia Island) meant a new word in my vocabulary, i.e., "resort casual."

Even though we have two resort subdivisions on the Island, "resort casual" is the dress code for all restaurants and venues, even the Jacksonville Symphony performances in nearby Jacksonville. Somehow, suits just don't fit in with this relaxed resort atmosphere, although pantsuits now seem fine for women.

Customers and clients came in to our office in shorts and sweatshirts all summer and jeans in winter. Realtors here tend to go for casual Izod shirts and khakis for guys and just about anything goes for women.

Speaking of dressing the part, I remember one of my first customers in Florida arrived in my office to sign a sales contract and asked if it was OK to bring her friend into the conference room. Of course, I agreed. When I looked up, I was greeted by an imposing tall black woman in some sort of native African dress.

Her hair, which I believe had never been cut, was twisted above her head in a loop and descended down into her shoulder bag. Her fingernails on one hand curled around in interesting sculptures and her dress was colorful and definitely not "business attire" or "resort casual."

This was my introduction to our Island's beloved "Beach Lady," MaVynne Betsch, an advocate for preserving NaNa, the great natural sand dune on American Beach, as well as being an advocate for other environmental and preservation causes.

Later I traveled to Tallahassee with her and others for a historical preservation grant to restore one of our African American schools. After many years that school became a community center, rather than an eyesore in our community.

Needless to say, clothes can make the man or woman, but in my job several of us went for comfortable skirts and short jackets or sweaters or pantsuits in the winter. Of course, when attending conferences and professional training out of the area, we all wore business suits.

To sum up, feeling comfortable is probably a good idea. Real estate agents spend a lot of time showing property, in and out of cars, putting up signs (watch out for red ant hills), leaning over to unlock lockboxes in the strangest places and even physically leaning up or staging a property for an open house. Did you see the movie *American Beauty* with Annette Benning? I don't recommend removing your suit top to clean before the open house, but I get it.

Therefore, comfort is a plus. Where I worked in Florida, it is also summer seven to eight months a year, another fine reason to be comfortable and casual.

Action Item 1 – Rule #18 – Ask a good friend to go through your closet with you after checking out what others wear in your area and your office policy.
Date_____

Rule #19 – Make Lots of Noise

Early in my career, I was always a little timid when showing homes. I would knock on the door or ring the doorbell, and quickly use the key or lockbox if no one answered. After two experiences, I began to be a little more boisterous and hesitate before barging in.

One occurred in Pittsburgh, where the sellers had assured me the house would still be empty. I knew there was no furniture there and that it had been vacant for quite a while, so I just did a little perfunctory bell ring and used the key. Imagine my surprise (and the buyers') when there was some scurrying and shrieks from the den or fourth bedroom to the right of the door when we entered.

I announced myself loudly, and we continued on in while the seller's daughter and boyfriend exited stage right to the garage. Now the real dilemma...do I report the incident when I call the sellers to give them feedback or stick to the buyers' reactions to the house and loose bedding on the floor?

I honestly don't remember exactly what I said, but the buyers laughed a lot and the sellers apologized when I called. Obviously, the daughter decided to tell Mom and Dad before I called.

The second incident occurred in Florida, when I was showing another supposedly vacant home on a busy street. I knocked on the door and used the lockbox key, but when I looked through the front glass door, I thought I saw some activity in the back of the house. I probably should have backed off with my clients, but I proceeded into the house noisily and told my clients to wait at the front door. When I reached the back door, which was open, someone was cycling down the driveway and there was another bicycle just sitting inside the door. I used my cell phone to call the listing agent, because, after all, it could have been the sellers taking their bikes or neighbors or something, and I left it up to her to report to the police, if needed.

Amazingly, the buyers thought this might be a high crime area, as it was on a main street and not really in a subdivision. They decided on another house.

Fortunately, both of these incidents ended up as funny stories, as did the one about the black snake and the beagle that bit my shoe....ask me sometime. But, this reminded me to think "safety first" and "announce your arrival" when showing homes.

....

Action Item 1 – Rule #19 – Make sure you lead clients into a house when showing property. Knock and ring the bell and always carry a cell phone for emergencies while showing as well.
Date_____

....

Rule #20 – Do Open Houses – Offer Ice Cream

I have to admit I only ever wrote one contract for the seller's house at an open house I was hosting, however, I do believe in holding them for other Realtors and the public.

As I started doing this in Pittsburgh, when I first moved there, I was lucky enough to have a walk-in listing on one of my early floor duty days. I certainly had no other customers at the time and this house was in a very high transient area where houses sold every three to four months.

The neighborhood was desirable and the traffic was heavy, which was great for me. No, I didn't sell that house from the open house, but my prospect list for buyers and sellers grew, and the house did sell, which could have been the result of the exposure.

I also remember doing an open house on the Northside in a model home and learned something from that experience as well. The builder paid for that ad, I got my name in the paper and I came home with a huge bump on my head. Beware of dining room chandeliers with no table underneath them. Fortunately, I did not break the chandelier.

Just some pointers on open houses: be prepared. Have a sign-in sheet (which you can explain your seller requires for visitors to his house) and, of course, this is a good security measure, should something disappear at the open house. Also, have brochures or listing copies of features in the house and data available for other homes available in the neighborhood or area as needed, a personal brochure, and your latest newsletter. Let the buyers know you are a professional. You do not have to give them all of this when they sign in, as they are normally anxious to see the house and avoid you. As they leave, you can ask them their impression of the house, what they are looking for, etc. and then hand them stuff as needed...or, if it is a really hot day, a nice ice cream cone or hot chocolate if it is cold and they will linger to talk.

You may get nosy neighbors, curious about the asking price. That is OK, as they could be future clients when the house you are sitting is sold.

Make sure you have a partner, licensed preferably (even ask a newbie in your office who has no business at all) or, at least, an assistant for safety's sake. That way one of you can always watch the door while the other accompanies the customers in case they have any questions.

I mentioned ice cream and hot chocolate, but my partner and I used to hold open houses, primarily for other Realtors at noon during the week and provide sandwiches and light lunch fare. This way if they haven't seen the house and are on the run, they can catch lunch at the same time. You may pick up some excellent comments from them, as well as exposure for your listing.

That brings us to advertising. I haven't talked about it much, but I remember a friend saying to me, "Wow, you must be doing great…I see your ads everywhere." I wasn't doing that great, but I was keeping my face, open houses and articles in the paper, as well as getting publicity for community activities. I think this helped make possible my image as a busy, professional Realtor.

....

Action Item 1 – Rule #20 – Plan an open house, ad in the paper.
Date_____

....

CHAPTER 5

Final Thoughts...Until the Next Book

Rule #21 – Be Ethical – Heed Your Conscience

"Realtor" is a copyrighted title and indicates that the agent belongs to his or her local, state, and National Association of Realtors. Therefore, the Realtor also subscribes to a national code of ethics and behavior guidelines.

All real estate agents or practitioners are not necessarily "Realtors," but, if they are, they can be held to the "Standards of Practice" listed in the "Code of Ethics," as well as the state laws that regulate our industry. However, even if an agent is not thinking about legal implications, he or she is aware of right and wrong.

For example, just treating customers, agents, and parties involved in a real estate transaction with respect and fairness should be a priority. Also, knowing the rules and guidelines for presenting mutiple offer contracts and the rules of agency (representation) in your state is a must.

I remember asking my usual question to new buyers in my office, "Are you working with any other agents? Have you been prequalified?" (Prequalified means meeting financial qualifications for a loan from a financial institution.)

They answered no and yes to those questions and we proceeded with discussing their real estate needs and desires. When I showed them one condo and two single-family homes near the office, they decided they really liked the last one best. We went back to the office to write up an offer. I could not believe how easy this day was going to be.

That's when I found out that they actually had seen this home before, but, according to them, the agent had not kept in touch, or returned their phone calls. After discussing the situation with them, I called the agent, whom I knew fairly well. He did not feel that he had abandoned them and had worked with them quite extensively. He came to our office, thanked me, and wrote up the offer.

Fortunately, I had not spent a lot of time and effort on that couple.

I have had cases when buyers did not want to work with another agent and that is a different situation.

In all the years I worked in the real estate industry, there were only a few times when I felt I had to rethink what was legally and morally right. In those instances discussing the situation with my broker, or, if needed, an attorney hot line provided by the Florida Association of Realtors, were good resources.

I even went to mediation in one instance, where I felt pretty strongly that my client would lose the case and had advised him all along that this could happen. Fortunately, I did not have to say much, as the attorney mostly questioned the sellers and buyers directly and interpreted the contract as he saw it.

Several people have asked me if the real estate community is really cutthroat. Honestly, I've heard of some incidents but did not find that to be an issue, although my husband tells me that I'm not very observant. I tend to keep my eyes on the road when I am driving, if you know what I mean. I have also been accused of being naïve and a Pollyanna type. I try to think the best of most people, so that could be true.

....

Action Item 1 – Rule #20 – Keep the Code of Ethics and Standards ready and read.
Date_____

....

Rule # 22 – Employ Your Relatives and Consult a Tax Specialist

I didn't have much experience with this rule personally, at least not in the way I should have. In other words, my husband worked for me for free. He was helpful and readily understood when I needed help.

However, one of the seminars I attended focused on how to employ your relatives and pay them legally while reaping tax benefits. Of course, if you have children with nothing better to do, this can either keep them busy or drive them into signing up for after-school activities. Just folding monthly newsletters or addressing mailings and Christmas cards can also be a good job for them.

Checking with a tax specialist when you start your business will also help you determine how to set it up tax wise and how family employees can be a beneficial tax deduction.

While consulting with a tax specialist, or real estate lawyer, you will need to decide how to set up your business practice, i.e., whether you will be an independent contractor, an s-corporation, an LLC, a partnership etc. Each setup has its own advantages and responsibilities.

As your own business, you will now also be responsible for paying quarterly taxes, another double burden as you will find out.

However, depending on how you are set up to do business, you may be able to reap all the profits.

....

Action Item I – Rule #22 – Consult with a real estate lawyer and/or tax consultant.
Date_____

....

Rule #23 – Take a Vacation – Have Some Fun

I still remember my husband's amazement at my suggestion for a break.

"You want to go where in February?" He swallowed.

"Austria," I said, summoning up lots of enthusiasm. "Imagine sleigh rides in the snow to the winter lodge, gondola rides to the top of the mountain ski areas, hot chocolate or warm cider on the train ride out to the country…"

My husband, who hates the cold and was the prime reason for our move from Seattle to Florida's warm weather, began to shake his head no.

"It's only $700 for a week in Innsbruck, airfare, hotel, and some meals included," I hastened to reply.

"That's quite a deal," he wavered. "How come it's so cheap?"

"Well, it's a package deal for a group of us Realtors, although we do have to fly from Jacksonville to Cincinnati to JFK airport in New York and on to Munich. Not only that, there are only a few spots left and the airfare just went down…whaddya say?"

So began our fun trip, our first real vacation since moving to Florida and my once again start-up career. We had a great time in Austria and got to know some of the Realtors and spouses in a casual and fun setting.

Although this was early in my Florida career, it helped me realize that short trips or vacations away help to relieve the high pressure of the real estate business, where time is money and instant responses are a necessity.

Over the years, we took a Caribbean cruise with a group from our dance club (about twenty of us). We also did another cruise with a group from the Jacksonville University Club. To top it all off, we arranged two family cruises to the Caribbean (a small group) and then to Bermuda with the whole family (seventeen of us). We even finished off our fun on large boats with a small group of friends to Mexico

As I got busier, it got harder to take time off, especially on weekends, our busy time. And, of course, as the pressure and business increased, that was the time I really needed a break from marketing, showing property, office duty, answering e-mails, keeping up Web sites, monitoring contracts for inspections, mortgage deadlines, insurance, and closing details.

Now it was only possible to take a weekend trip here and there. Have you ever been to Hastings, the potato capital of Florida, or Micanopy, the antique markets center? You don't have to travel all the way to Savannah, St. Augustine, Charleston, or Orlando to have some time away. In fact, we even managed a weekend trip occasionally on our motorboat with the sail club or just a quick trip up to Cumberland Island to get a break from the hectic routine.

These times are especially necessary for birthdays, anniversaries, and family occasions. So remember to actually write them on your schedule, not just your business appointments.

I actually ended up with two calendars, one at home for social engagements and one in the office for business events. However, I had both on my Palm Pilot to check before commiting to anything.

I think I might not have retired, even though I was sixty-three, if I had planned my working hours better. In other words, I would have been less stressed if I had taken regular vacations, exercise classes, or time off.

Writing down time for a weekend off, or nights for dinner out, even a day trip in your planner or iPhone, as if they were business appointments can keep you from feeling overwhelming pressure with time constraints. I worked days, nights, and weekends and put clients first for a long time. Finally, I started keeping Sundays for the family and me and it really helped.

I remember taking "Curves" classes one year at 7:30 in the morning, three times a week and just showing up a little later those days. I felt much better prepared for work and physically better as well.

Action Item 1 – Rule #23 – Commit to family dates.
Date_____

Action Item 2 – Rule #23 – Plan a vacation.
Date_____

Rule #24 – Attending the Home Inspection – Yes or No

There are two trains of thought on whether or not the buyer's agent should attend the home inspection. A top producer in one of my offices felt it was better not to be there. When I asked why, she replied, "That way I am not liable in any way for the results of the inspection, meaning what the home inspector may or may not have said at the inspection. The written report is what we go by."

I saw the validity of this point of view. On the other hand, I felt that I needed to stand by my buyer, if I represented him and especially if he requested it. I could be aware of questions that came up were unanswered, or concerns of the buyer.

I once had a seller ask me to attend the home inspection, but as the buyer was paying for the inspection and was to be there, the buyer did not feel it was appropriate and I was just as happy not to be there. However, I have been present as the seller's or the buyer's agent when I was the only one available to let the inspector in to the house. In fact, that was the strangest home inspection I ever went on for the buyer, who was not in Florida at the time. I opened the house at the front door, while the inspector began to walk around the outside of the house visibly checking the condition and making notes. I expected him inside shortly and was turning on lights, etc., when I realized he was taking a long time and thought he might have decided to walk the roof. So, I headed outside as he walked toward me from the side yard. A red crease stood out across his forehead. When I asked him about it, he said that he hadn't realized the lintel or top on the gate to the fenced yard was so short and was taking pictures as he walked through it, virtually knocking himself out when he hit it with his forehead.

Most of the home inspectors don't knock themselves out doing the job, but this became a joke between us for a long time. He is now retired, so I think I can tell it.

I remember in the '70s when very few buyers had complete inspections. In fact, buyers might bring a father or friend in construction along before they wrote the contract, or even make that a condition of the contract. Most of the transactions then were really based on the phrase, "buyer beware."

The age of consumer awareness, resulted in the current situation where many state contracts include provisions for all kind of inspection, i.e., energy efficiency, general home inspection, termite and radon inspections, just to name a few. Also, as mentioned before, the seller's disclosure statement is often included in contracts today.

....

Action Item I – Rule #24 – Discuss home inspections with broker/buyers.
Date_____

....

Rule #25 – Know When to Retire

I used to want to live and work in the same town forever, then retire like my dad and my parents' generation. Then you get to do whatever you want...travel...read...cruise the Great Circle Loop of the Eastern United State on your trawler with hundreds of other retirees (my husband's dream).

In reality, I think our generation has done things differently. We move around from job to job, state to state. We take big vacations whenever we want and can afford to do so. And, in truth, I certainly have had an interesting life, while working hard.

We've been on many cruises alone or with family and friends, including one to Alaska. We've traveled around the US on vacation to visit friends and have even been overseas to England, France, Austria, and Spain. We boated the San Juan and Gulf Islands in the Pacific Northwest. In the last three years I worked in real estate we boated up and down the Eastern United States, at which time, I took a real estate partner to keep me involved in the business while I was away.

My partner and I both did well with this arrangement, and I truly recommend this route when you are doing well and overworked. However, the last boat trip on our trawler in 2007 took eight months to do the whole Loop (see www.tomclare.com). I just couldn't see myself back in the office and in real estate again. It was almost like starting over again. So, nearing my Social Security benefit, I decided to use my license for referrals only and got my real estate instructor's license to teach the licensing course. I also taught some training classes for one broker.

But, I think I really saw signs that it was time to retire, when I started getting annoyed with buyers, other agents, and some of my sellers, as well. Maybe getting older makes you have less patience? Whatever the reason, I was definitely ready to do something else, and, no, I did not know the market was going into decline in 2007.

Action Item 1 – Rule #25 – Plan for retirement.
Date: Now

Action Item 2 – Rule #25 – Consult family, taxman, and social security for financial consequences of retirement.
Date:_____

www.ingramcontent.com/pod-product-compliance
Lightning Source LLC
Chambersburg PA
CBHW071801040426
42446CB00012B/2655